The Fun Fa... VIOLIN Book

by Katie Elliott
with Anthony Marks

Illustrations by Ian Martin
Illustrations © Copyright 1998 by Boosey & Hawkes Music Publishers Ltd.

BOOSEY & HAWKES

London · New York · Berlin · Sydney

© Copyright 1998 by Katie Elliott

Welcome to the Fun Factory Violin Book!

A quick introduction!
A look at the different parts of the violin and a guide to what they do. **p.3**

The violin family.
A guide to some of the most important members of the violin family. **p.4**

Around the world.
An introduction to some of the different kinds of violin played around the world. **p.6**

How a violin works.
How is a sound produced? Why is the violin the shape and size it is? **p.8**
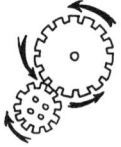

Violin-making.
A look at the many different processes involved in making a violin. **p.10**

Owning a violin.
Advice on buying a violin and helpful hints about how to take care of it. **p.12**

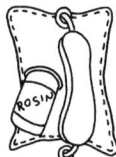
The best instrument?
Love it or hate it, everyone has an opinion. What do people think of the violin? **p.14**

Design and invention.
How has the design of the violin changed throughout history? **p.16**

Music and musicians.
A look at the history of violin music and the people who played it. **p.18**

The violin's repertoire.
Suggestions of some famous violin pieces which you might like to listen to. **p.20**

A violinist's life.
Fame and fortune, or hard work and stage fright? What is it like to be a violinist? **p.22**

What can I do next?
Hints to help you become a better violinist, plus fun ideas and things to do. **p.24**

Problems and advice.
Worried? Need someone to talk to? Then this is definitely the page for you... **p.26**

The violin A to Z.
A set of violin facts - some interesting, some fun, and some downright silly! **p.28**

Useful information.
A guide to some of the most common words and signs used in music. **p.30**

The back page.
Can't find what you're looking for? Maybe an index and answers section will help! **p.32**

A quick introduction.

A look at the different parts of the violin and a guide to what they do.

About this book...

This is a book for anyone who is interested in finding out about the violin. It doesn't matter whether you play already, are thinking about learning, or just want to know more - there's something for everyone. Have fun!

Parts of the violin

The violin looks quite simple, but it has over 70 different parts. Some of the main ones are shown here. You can find out more about how violins work on page 8, and how they are built on page 10.

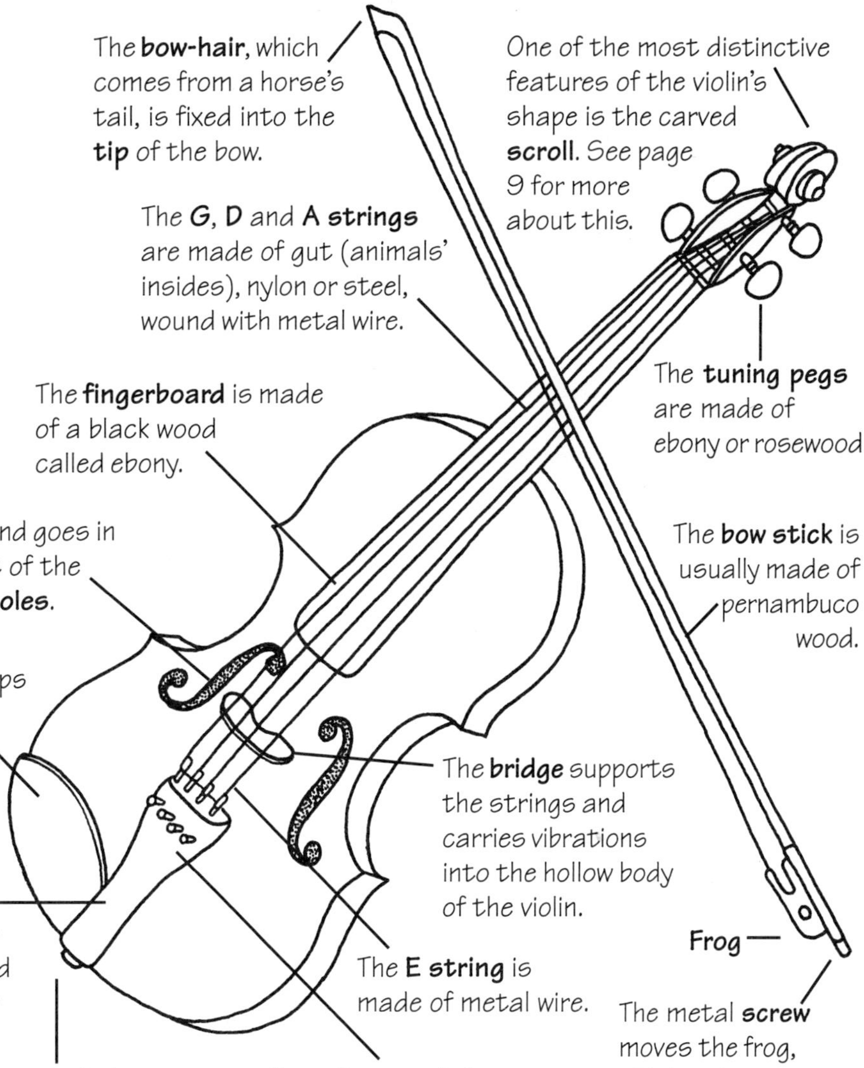

The **bow-hair**, which comes from a horse's tail, is fixed into the **tip** of the bow.

The **G**, **D** and **A strings** are made of gut (animals' insides), nylon or steel, wound with metal wire.

The **fingerboard** is made of a black wood called ebony.

The sound goes in and out of the **soundholes**.

The **chin-rest** helps you hold the violin between your neck and your shoulder.

The **tailpiece** holds the strings in place. It is fixed to the end-pin by nylon or gut.

The **end-pin** keeps the tailpiece in place.

One of the most distinctive features of the violin's shape is the carved **scroll**. See page 9 for more about this.

The **tuning pegs** are made of ebony or rosewood.

The **bow stick** is usually made of pernambuco wood.

The **bridge** supports the strings and carries vibrations into the hollow body of the violin.

The **E string** is made of metal wire.

Frog

The metal **screw** moves the frog, which tightens or loosens the bow-hair.

The **adjusters** help you tune the strings.

The violin family.

A guide to some of the most important members of the violin family.

Shapes and sizes

The violin is the smallest of the stringed instruments found in an orchestra. The body of a full-size violin is roughly 35.5 cm long, has four strings (the lowest of which is tuned to the G below middle C) and a range of about 3½ octaves. You can find out much more about the violin in the rest of the book, but first here's some information about its closest relatives - the viola, cello and double bass.

Viola

The viola is larger than the violin, and can be up to 10cm longer. The lowest of its four strings is tuned to the C below middle C. Like the violin, the viola also has a range of roughly 3½ octaves, but its tone is mellower.

Before the 18th century, composers rarely wrote separate lines of music for the violas. They had to play the same music as the cellos or basses.

After that time, composers began to write separate parts for violas, and the instrument became a vital part of the symphony orchestra and the string quartet (see page 21 for more about this).

Viola music is usually written in a special clef called the alto clef, shown here. When you see it in music, it means that the note on the middle line of the staff is middle C.

⚠️ Before the early 16th century, the word "viola" referred to many different instruments. It simply meant "a stringed instrument played with a bow".

Violoncello

The full name of the cello is "violoncello". The lowest of its four strings is tuned to the C two octaves below middle C, and it has a range of around 3½ octaves. The body of a full-size cello is about 75cm long.

The first cellos were built at the end of the 16th century. The instrument became very popular in orchestras, and in smaller groups too.

The cello is held between the player's knees. In the mid-19th century, a metal spike called an end-pin was added, so that the instrument could be rested on the floor.

Most cello music is written in the bass clef, but the tenor clef (shown below) and treble clef can also be used for higher notes. The tenor clef tells you that the note on the second highest line of the staff is middle C.

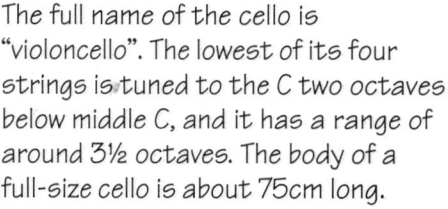
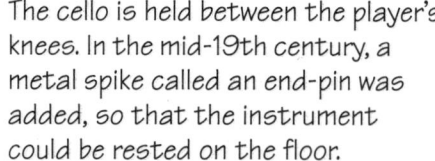
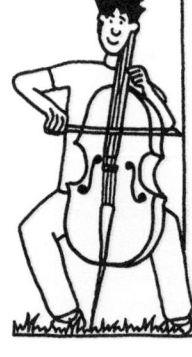

Double Bass

The double bass is the largest and lowest pitched member of the violin family. Its lowest string is E, nearly three octaves below middle C. It has a range of about 2½ octaves.

Because the double bass is such a large instrument its strings are tuned in fourths, not fifths like the rest of the violin family. This makes the fingering easier.

The double bass has been a regular member of the orchestra since the 18th century. It is also commonly used in jazz and pop music - much more so than violins, violas or cellos.

Double basses vary in size and shape more than almost any other instrument. The commonest size is about 115cm in length, but double basses can be much taller than this. Some people sit on a stool to play; others prefer to stand up.

 Double bass music is usually written an octave higher than the actual sound. This avoids having to write too many notes on ledger lines below the stave.

Things to listen to...

There are interesting **viola** parts in many string quartets (see page 21), particularly those by Mozart and Brahms. Look out also for concertos by Hindemith and Bartók.

If you want to listen to **cello** music, you could try the concertos by Elgar and Dvorak, or unaccompanied works such as the Six Suites for Solo Cello by J.S. Bach.

A very famous example of music for the **double bass** is "The Elephant", from Saint-Saëns' "Carnival of the Animals". It is also featured in all kinds of jazz, especially music by bass players such as Charles Mingus.

 The largest known double bass was made to celebrate the 1889 Cincinnati music festival by a man named Paul de Wit. It is 4.8 metres high!

Really BAD Ideas!

There are lots of great things to do with a violin, but this is **not** one of them . . .

1. Leaving it somewhere where it will get very hot . . . or very cold.

Around the world.

An introduction to some of the different kinds of violin played around the world.

All shapes and sizes!

When we think about violins, we usually imagine the sort of instrument shown on page 3. But there are lots of other bowed stringed instruments which are also close relatives of the violin.

- Some have short necks and are held under the chin or against the player's chest. Others have long necks and are held between the player's knees (like a cello) or resting on the floor (like a double bass).

- Some have just one string, others have many. Some have "sympathetic strings", which are not played with the bow. The vibration of the bowed strings makes them sound at the same time.

- Instruments like these are commonly used to play different types of folk music all over the world. Because of this, they are often described as "folk fiddles".

Quick Fit!

Can you fit the names of the folk fiddles listed below into the grid? Place them correctly and read down the starred squares to find the name of another instrument - this time from Bulgaria.

Now all you need to do is read the descriptions below to find out more about each of these weird and wonderful fiddles from around the world.

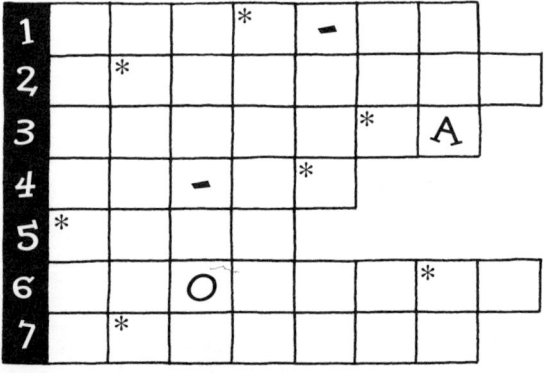

ER-HU   MASENQO   WANG-PI   LIRA
SARINDA   KAMANCHA   ZLOBCOKI

1. A Tibetan instrument played with a bow made from a yak's tail.
2. A kind of folk fiddle played in many countries including Iran and Algeria.
3. An Indian instrument with a distinctive round-bodied shape.
4. A Chinese two-string violin with a snakeskin-covered body.
5. A Greek folk fiddle with a wide neck and a pear-shaped body.
6. A fiddle used to play Polish folk music.
7. An Ethiopian one-string fiddle with a diamond-shaped body.

Cacti and clogs

Folk fiddles are not only made from wood. All sorts of materials are used, including thick card, old tin cans, hollowed out fruit shells and cactus stalks, and pieces of animal skin. For bows, the fibre from coconut trees or palm leaves is sometimes used.

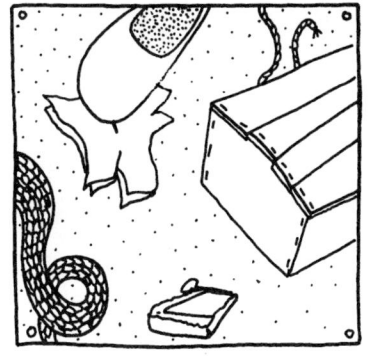

 The 'kloompviol' from the Netherlands is a fiddle made from a wooden clog with strings stretched across it.

The morin khuur

In Mongolia, desert nomads play a long-necked fiddle called a morin khuur. The scroll and peg-box are carved in the shape of a horse's head. It has two strings, one thin and one thick, and is played with a horsehair bow.

 The first morin khuur is said to have been made from the remains of a horse featured in Mongolian folk tales.

The sarangi

The sarangi is played in northern India and Pakistan. It has three or four bowed strings, as well as a varying number of sympathetic strings. It is used both to accompany singers, and as a solo instrument too.

 The sarangi can have up to four bridges. Traditionally, one of these is carved in the shape of an elephant.

The Hardanger fiddle

In western Norway, the Hardanger fiddle has been popular for centuries. It looks quite like an ordinary violin but is highly decorated, especially on the fingerboard, pegbox and tailpiece. It has four or five sympathetic strings which are fixed below the fingerboard.

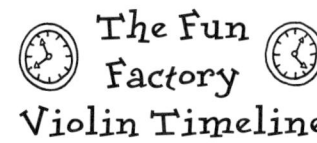

The Fun Factory Violin Timeline

The Fun Factory Violin Timeline is a list of dates in the history of the violin, plus information about famous people, inventions, discoveries and lots more.

(The letter 'c' stands for the Latin word 'circa', which means 'about'.)

⇩

c.65 million B.C. Dinosaurs become extinct.

⇩

c.200,000 B.C. Modern man (known as 'homo sapiens') evolves in Africa.

⇩

c.40,000 B.C. People begin to use bones to make simple whistles.

⇩

c.3,500 B.C. The first wheels are made.

⇩

c.2,560 B.C. After many years in construction, the Great Pyramid at Giza in Egypt is finally completed.

⇩

c.1600 B.C. People begin to use an early form of the alphabet we know today.

⇩

776 B.C. The first Olympic Games are held in Greece.

⇩

How a violin works.

How is a sound produced? Why is the violin the shape and size it is?

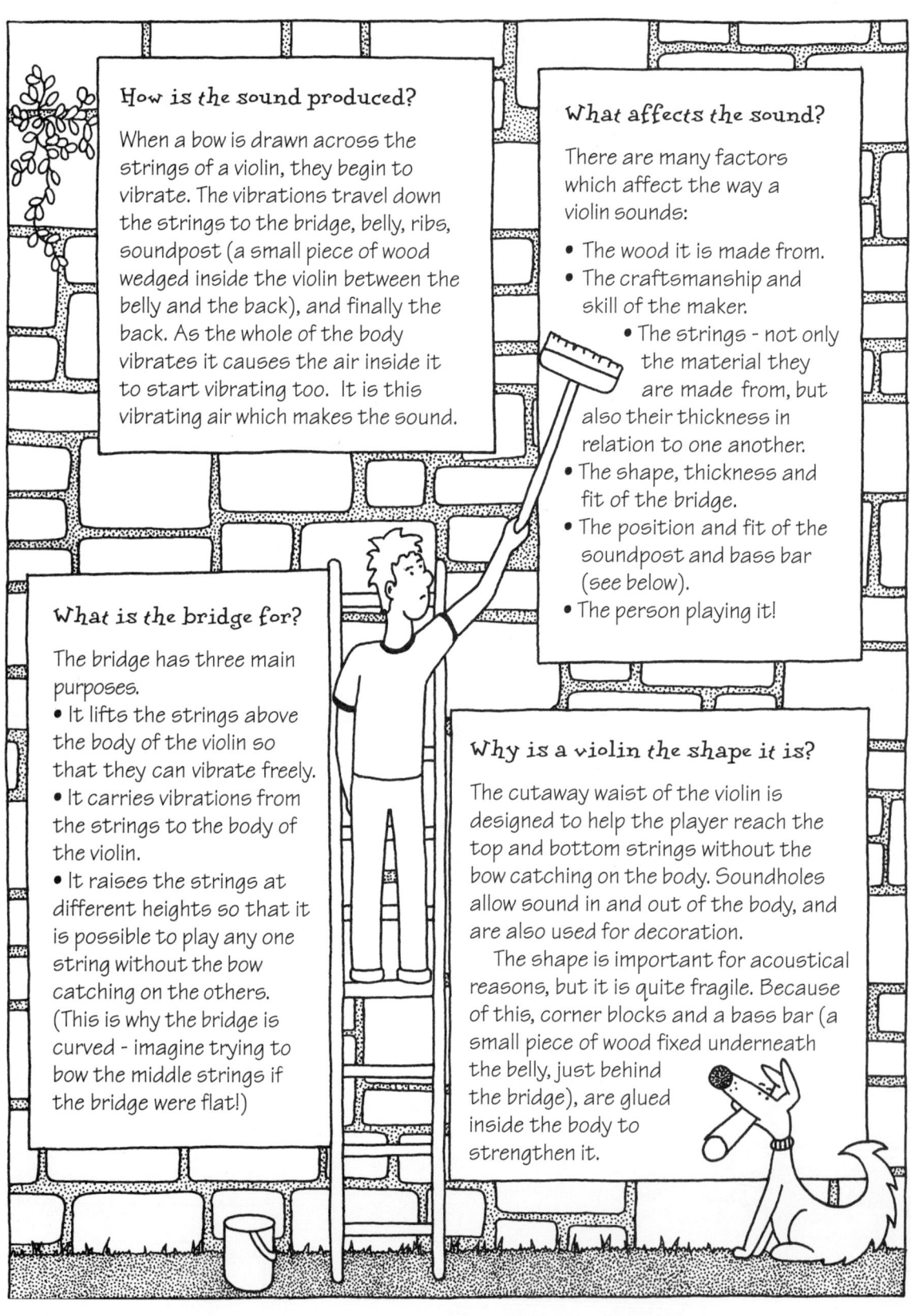

How is the sound produced?

When a bow is drawn across the strings of a violin, they begin to vibrate. The vibrations travel down the strings to the bridge, belly, ribs, soundpost (a small piece of wood wedged inside the violin between the belly and the back), and finally the back. As the whole of the body vibrates it causes the air inside it to start vibrating too. It is this vibrating air which makes the sound.

What affects the sound?

There are many factors which affect the way a violin sounds:

- The wood it is made from.
- The craftsmanship and skill of the maker.
- The strings - not only the material they are made from, but also their thickness in relation to one another.
- The shape, thickness and fit of the bridge.
- The position and fit of the soundpost and bass bar (see below).
- The person playing it!

What is the bridge for?

The bridge has three main purposes.
- It lifts the strings above the body of the violin so that they can vibrate freely.
- It carries vibrations from the strings to the body of the violin.
- It raises the strings at different heights so that it is possible to play any one string without the bow catching on the others. (This is why the bridge is curved - imagine trying to bow the middle strings if the bridge were flat!)

Why is a violin the shape it is?

The cutaway waist of the violin is designed to help the player reach the top and bottom strings without the bow catching on the body. Soundholes allow sound in and out of the body, and are also used for decoration.

The shape is important for acoustical reasons, but it is quite fragile. Because of this, corner blocks and a bass bar (a small piece of wood fixed underneath the belly, just behind the bridge), are glued inside the body to strengthen it.

Are violins always made of wood?

No. Some violin makers have tried using different materials (such as metals and carbon fibre), but so far none of these have been as successful as wood. Wood is good for violin making for many reasons - it is light, easy to work, resonant and attractive to look at.

What is the scroll used for?

Nowadays, the scroll is mainly a decorative feature. Makers use different shapes and designs of scroll as a way of personalizing their violins. But in the past the scroll had a more practical purpose. Violinists used to hang their instruments up by it when they finished playing!

Are old violins always the best?

Not necessarily. Some of the oldest Italian violins (see pages 16-17), are thought to be among the best ever made. They are certainly the most valuable! But tests show that it can actually be hard to tell the difference in sound between these violins and modern ones.

Really BAD Ideas!

There are lots of great things to do with a violin, but this is <u>not</u> one of them . . .

2. Messing about with it.

Timeline 650BC-105AD

c.650 B.C. People begin to use coins for trading.

c.563 B.C. Siddharta Gautama, founder of Buddhism, is born in India.

c.550 B.C. 'Aesop's Fables' are written.

c.300 B.C. The 'Mahabharata', thought to be the world's longest poem, is completed.

c.250 B.C. The first organ is built. It uses water power to make a sound.

c.214 B.C. The Great Wall of China is completed. It is approximately 6,500 kilometres long.

c.45 B.C. Caesar becomes ruler of the Roman Empire.

c.30 A.D. The founder of Christianity, Jesus of Nazareth, is crucified.

105 A.D. In China, people discover a way of making paper.

Violin-making.

A look at the many different processes involved in making a violin.

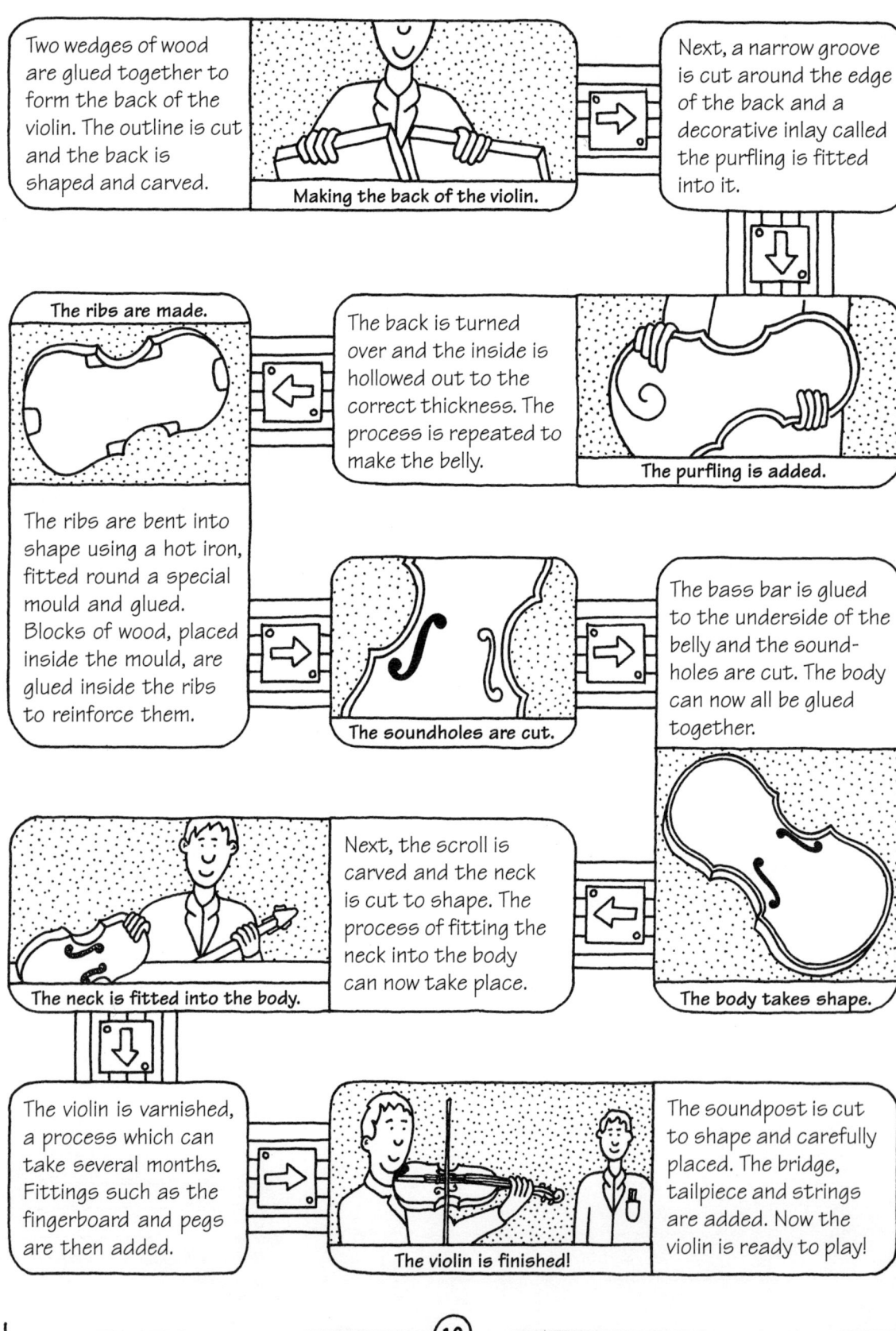

Quick Code!

Here are some facts about materials used in violin-making - but some of the information is in code! Translate it using the code: 1 = A, 2 = B, 3 = C and so on. (You can use the space at the foot of the page if you want to write out the code in full.)

The back of the violin is made from a hard wood such as _ _ _ _ _ (13-1-16-12-5). The ribs and scroll are often made from this too.

The belly and the soundpost are made from a soft wood such as _ _ _ _ _ _ (19-16-18-21-3-5). This is because soft woods carry vibrations better than hard ones.

A strong, dark wood called _ _ _ _ _ (5-2-15-14-25) is used to make the fingerboard, saddle, tailpiece and pegs. Violin makers use it because it is both attractive to look at and hardwearing.

The hair used in violin bows is taken from the tail of a _ _ _ _ _ (8-15-18-19-5). Synthetic materials have been tried, but it seems that natural hair is best for the job.

The bow stick is made from _ _ _ _ _ _ _ _ _ _ (16-5-18-14-1-13-2-21-3-15) wood, from Brazil. It has just the right combination of flexibility and density to make it suitable for bow-making.

A hardwearing synthetic material such as _ _ _ _ _ _ _ (16-12-1-19-20-9-3) is generally used to make the chin-rest.

....
....
....
....

Timeline 570-1550

570 The religious leader Mohammed is born in Mecca, in the country now called Saudi Arabia.

c.860 In China, printing techniques are developed. The first book is printed.

c.1156 The Kremlin is built in Moscow.

1387 The poet Geoffrey Chaucer writes 'The Canterbury Tales'.

1473 In Germany, music is printed for the first time.

1492 Columbus arrives in America.

c.1505 Andrea Amati, one of the world's first great violin makers, is born.

1522 The 'Vittoria' becomes the first ship to sail around the world.

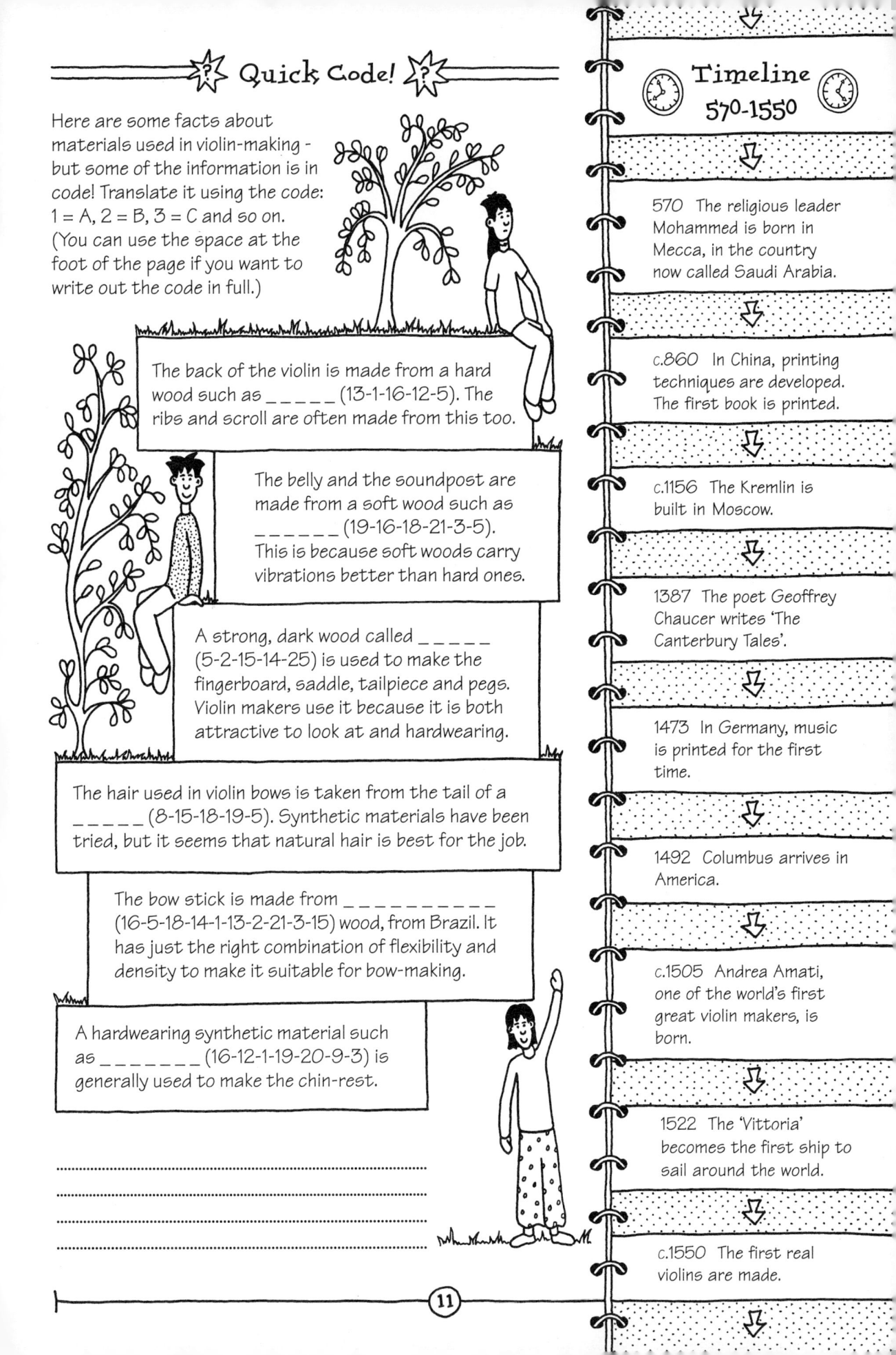

c.1550 The first real violins are made.

Owning a violin.

Advice on buying a violin and helpful hints about how to take care of it.

Whether you are choosing your very first violin or replacing your old one, you need to think carefully before deciding which to buy. It's a good idea to ask someone who knows about violins to advise you - your teacher is probably the best person to help.

Things to think about when choosing your violin...

Which size?
Violins come in several different sizes so you should ask your teacher which one you will need - this will depend on how big you are, and how fast you are growing. Whichever size you choose, it's very important that the violin should feel comfortable for you to hold.

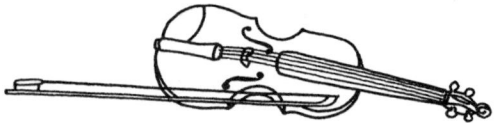

New or second-hand?
You can buy new violins at a wide range of prices. The cheaper ones can be fine for beginners. Remember that a new violin takes a while to "play in" (settle down after manufacture). If you buy a second-hand violin, it may sound better and be better value for money. But look out for damage - some cracks in the wood don't matter, but others can be serious. Always ask for advice before buying. (And remember that an old violin is not always better than a new one.)

What next?
The set-up of your violin will need to be checked, perhaps by your teacher, or by someone in a violin shop. The height of the bridge, shape of the chinrest and type of strings may need to be changed so that you feel really comfortable. Check that the case is tough enough to protect your instrument but light enough to carry easily.

What else will you need?
Rosin: this helps the bow to grip the strings.
Dusters: you need one very soft duster to wrap your violin up in (a silk scarf is a good idea), and another one - not too fluffy! - for cleaning it after you finish playing.
Shoulder pad: your teacher will help you to choose one of these.

Really BAD Ideas!
There are lots of great things to do with a violin, but this is <u>not</u> one of them...

3. Forgetting where you left it...

How to take care of your violin.

When you finish playing, use a soft duster to remove any rosin dust from the strings, the fingerboard, and around the bridge (be gentle!). Wipe away any fingermarks from the wood, too.

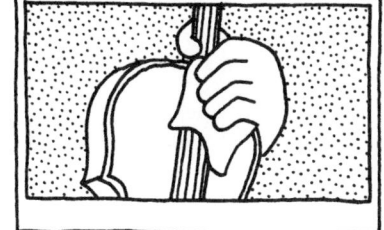

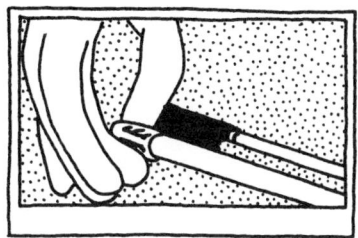

Loosen the bow-hair slightly by turning the screw. Next shake the bow very gently, and use the duster to remove any rosin dust from the stick. Then carefully put the violin and bow back in the case.

Quick Workout!

Four young violinists have been out shopping. They've all come home with something new - but can you work out what? Read the statements below and see if you can deduce how old each violinist is, and what each one has bought. Then write your answers in the grid below. Happy puzzling!

NAME	AGE	PURCHASE

1. **Jenny** bought the **rosin** to replace some she lost at school.
2. **Marco** is a year younger than the girl who bought a new **violin**, but two years older than his little brother **Richard**.
3. It was the youngest shopper who went with his dad to choose a **bow** - not the **13** year old.
4. **Dominique** (who is **11**), didn't buy the **duster** or the **bow**.

Timeline 1595-1756

c.1595 Shakespeare writes 'Romeo and Juliet'.

1608 Dutch scientist Hans Lippershey invents the telescope.

c.1653 The Taj Mahal is built at Agra in India.

c. 1666 Antonio Stradivari goes to work for Nicolo Amati and begins to make violins.

c.1709 In Italy, Bartolommeo Cristofori builds the first piano.

1719 Daniel Defoe finishes writing the novel 'Robinson Crusoe' about the life of a shipwrecked sailor.

1725 Vivaldi composes 'The Four Seasons'.

1737 Stradivari makes his last violin. He dies later in the same year.

1756 The world's first chocolate factory is opened.

The best instrument?

Love it or hate it, everyone has an opinion. What do people think of the violin?

Those in favour...

Throughout history, famous people have praised the violin for many different reasons:

- **Hector Berlioz (1803-1869) liked using violins in his compositions. He regarded them as "faithful, intelligent, active and indefatigable servants."**

- In his book 'Harmonie universelle' (1636), the French music writer Marin Mersenne was even more enthusiastic, describing the violin as "the king of musical instruments".

- **And author Jeremy Collier (1650-1726) was amazed that a simple instrument could affect those who listened to it so deeply. He wrote: "What can be more strange than that the rubbing of a little hair and cat-gut together should make such a mighty alteration in a man that sits at a distance?"**

...and those against.

Not everyone thinks highly of the violin though - some people don't like it at all!

- **The writer Thomas Mace described the sound of the violin as "High Priz'd Noise, fit to make a Man's Ears Glow, and fill his Brains full of Frisks..." (1676).**

- In his novel 'A Christmas Carol', Dickens complained that the sound of a violinist tuning up was "like fifty stomach aches".

- **When compiling his dictionary, Ambrose Bierce defined the violin as "an instrument to tickle human ears by friction of a horse's tail on the entrails of a cat."**

- In 1749, Lord Chesterfield wrote to his son warning him not to develop a taste for "fiddling and piping" as it would lead him into "bad company"!

Quick Riddle!

Solve the riddle to find the name of a composer who wrote a famous piece for the violin. (See page 20 to find out more!)

My first's in **technique** and it's also in **tone**
My next's not in **solo**, though it is in **alone**
My third is in **string** and in **wire**, but not **gut**
My fourth's not in **bridge**, but in **chinrest** and **nut**
My fifth is in **teaching** as well as **advice**
My sixth's not in **grip**, but in **fingering** (twice!)
My seventh's in **jig**, and it's also in **fiddle**
So look at the clues and unravel my riddle!

The mystery composer is ....

I'm glad I play the violin because...

We asked you to tell us why you like playing the violin. Here are some of the things you said:

...it means I can play a solo in the school concert.

...when I practise it makes my dog howl!

...I can join the youth orchestra with my friends.

...there are lots and lots of different kinds of music to play.

...it's easier to carry than a double bass!

Timeline 1776-1820

1776 On July 4th, the people of North America declare independence from Great Britain.

1783 The Montgolfier brothers make the first flight in a hot-air balloon.

c.1785 Tourte designs the kind of bow used today.

1789 George Washington becomes the first ever president of America.

1791 Wolfgang Amadeus Mozart completes his opera 'The Magic Flute'.

1795 Paganini makes his first tour, aged just 13.

1806 Beethoven's violin concerto is first performed. It is thought to be very difficult to play.

1814 Inventor Johann Maelzel patents the clockwork metronome.

1820 People begin to use stamps to send letters.

Design and invention.

How has the design of the violin changed throughout history?

The earliest violins

It is hard to say when the very first violin was made. The instrument developed over many years from other stringed instruments - such as the ancient *lira da braccio* and *rebec*. The violin is also thought to be related to the *viol*, a different branch of the stringed instrument family. Early violins were certainly in use by the middle of the 16th century. However at first they only had three strings and were held against the arm or the chest, rather than the shoulder as they are today.

The first known pictures of the new instrument were painted in 1535 on the ceiling of Saronno cathedral in Italy by the artist Gaudenzio Ferrari. They show angels playing a violin, a viola and a cello.

Famous city, famous names

Cremona, in northern Italy, quickly became the centre of violin making. The first important maker was Andrea Amati, who lived from around 1505 to 1580. His grandson Nicolo (1596-1684) was the most famous member of the family. Nicolo's pupils included Andreas Guarneri and Antonio Stradivari (see opposite). These people created some of the finest violins ever made, continually improving the instrument by experimenting with different woods and designs.

One reason Cremona violins were special is their varnish. It was not a secret at the time, but when later makers found quicker ways of varnishing instruments the Cremona methods were lost, and now no-one knows exactly what they were.

Changes and modernization

After the deaths of the last great Italian violin makers Stradivari (1737) and Giuseppe Antonio Guarneri (known as "del Gesù", 1744), France gradually became the centre of violin making. French makers like Nicolas Lupot (1758-1824) made a number of changes to the structure of the instrument, making it stronger and slightly larger. These changes gave it a more powerful sound, better suited to playing in the larger concert halls which were being built at the time.

Other developments

By 1800, the violin had reached a standard shape and structure. The major innovation around this time was a new kind of bow, perfected in France by François Tourte. Tourte made the bow curve in rather than outwards, and built it out of lighter wood. This made it more flexible and easier to control. Old-style "arch" bows quickly went out of fashion, and few of them are left today.

Another development was the invention of the chin-rest in about 1820, by Ludwig Spohr. This enabled the player to hold the instrument firmly between his or her chin and shoulder.

There have been few changes in violin design since this time. New shapes and materials have been tried, but the traditionally made wooden violin still remains by far the most popular.

STRADIVARI-FILE

Who was he?
Antonio Stradivari (1644-1737) was one of the greatest violin makers of all time. He spent the whole of his life in Cremona, making his last violin there at the age of 92.

What did he do?
During his lifetime he made around 1200 instruments. He specialized in violins, however he occasionally made violas and cellos as well. His instruments were always superbly designed and constructed, and many of them were also beautifully decorated.

About 600 of Stradivari's instruments are still in existence. The best ones have a powerful but sweet tone, and are easy to play. Many of them are nicknamed after the famous violinists who owned them in the past, such as Viotti and Rode. Nowadays instruments by Stradivari are bought and sold for millions of pounds.

Timeline 1820-1878

c.1820 Louis Spohr invents the chin-rest.

1846 A Belgian named Adolphe Sax designs the saxophone.

1848 The great Gold Rush begins in California.

1865 Lewis Carroll writes the story of 'Alice's Adventures in Wonderland'.

1867 Alfred Nobel patents dynamite, after inventing it by accident!

1874 After working on them for 24 years, Wagner completes his 'Ring Cycle' of operas.

1876 Bell patents his designs for a telephone.

1877 The first ever Wimbledon Tennis Championship takes place.

1878 The composer Peter Ilyich Tchaikovsky finishes writing his violin concerto.

Music and musicians.

A look at the history of violin music and the people who played it.

Dancing and singing

By 1600, the violin had become popular all over Europe. In France it was mostly used to play dance music at social occasions. The parts were generally quite simple and played from memory rather than written down. In Italy and Germany, the violin was also important in vocal music, both in church and elsewhere.

In the 17th century, many rich people liked to play the viol as a hobby. They dismissed the violin as a common instrument, played only by poor people who had to work in orchestras or at court to earn a living.

Composer-violinists

Gradually a new style of violin music developed in Italy. It began with Arcangelo Corelli (1653-1713), a violinist who began writing pieces that made a feature of the special sound of the instrument. For the first time, the violin had its own music which displayed both the instrument's qualities and the performer's skill.

Corelli developed new types of piece - sonatas for single instrument and accompaniment, trio sonatas (two instruments and accompaniment) and concerto grosso (a large piece for several groups of instruments).

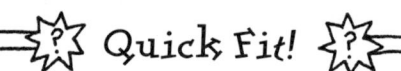

Quick Fit!

Here's some more information about the history of the violin. Can you work out which of the words in the box fit into each of the spaces below?

During the .... and 19th ...., the violin's

popularity .... As performers became more

............., composers began to write more ....

showpieces for them to play. .... such as

.... (see opposite) and Joachim became

superstars. Huge .... flocked to their

.... to marvel at their virtuoso ....

Suddenly it was very .... to play the ....!

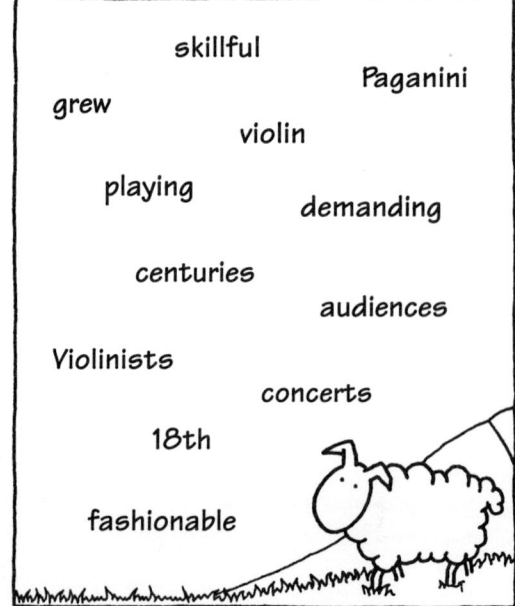

skillful
Paganini
grew
violin
playing
demanding
centuries
audiences
Violinists
concerts
18th
fashionable

PAGANINI-FILE

Who was he?
Niccolò Paganini (1782-1840) was born in Genoa, Italy. He is thought to have been the greatest virtuoso violinist of the 19th century.

What did he do?
He made his first public appearance as a violinist at the age of 10, and by 13 was touring as a soloist. In 1805 he wrote his 24 Caprices for unaccompanied violin, which became his most famous composition. These pieces used many "special effects" like artificial harmonics, left-hand pizzicato and unusual bowing patterns. These techniques are now common, but at the time they revolutionised violin playing. Audiences were amazed at Paganini's skill, which brought him fame all over Europe and made the violin enormously popular.

Paganini's compositions included concertos, string quartets and solo pieces. He was also a fine guitarist, and wrote guitar music too.

The modern violin.

The pursuit of technical excellence continued in the 20th century with violinists such as Fritz Kreisler and Jascha Heifetz. Today, players continue to explore new techniques. Some experiment to find ways of producing new sounds from a traditional violin. Others work with amplification and electronic instruments such as the MIDI violin instead.

The violin continues to play a very important role in classical music, both as a solo instrument, and in groups such as the string quartet and the orchestra.

It is used in other styles of music as well. For example, players such as Stephane Grappelli and Jean-Luc Ponty have helped to make the violin a recognized jazz instrument. It is commonly used in pop, and is an essential part of much of the world's folk music too.

Timeline 1880-1925

1880 The French sculptor Auguste Rodin produces the first designs for his sculpture 'The Thinker'.

1889 French engineer, Gustave Eiffel, builds the Eiffel Tower in Paris.

1903 The first successful petrol-powered flight.

1904 J. M. Barrie's best-known book, 'Peter Pan', is published.

1908 French jazz violinist, Stephane Grappelli, is born.

1913 Stravinsky writes 'The Rite of Spring'.

1914 World War I begins. Before long 16 nations are involved in the fighting. It lasts until 1918.

1917 Jascha Heifetz makes his U.S. debut at the Carnegie Hall aged 17.

1925 John Logie Baird invents the television.

The violin's repertoire.

Suggestions of some famous violin pieces which you might like to listen to.

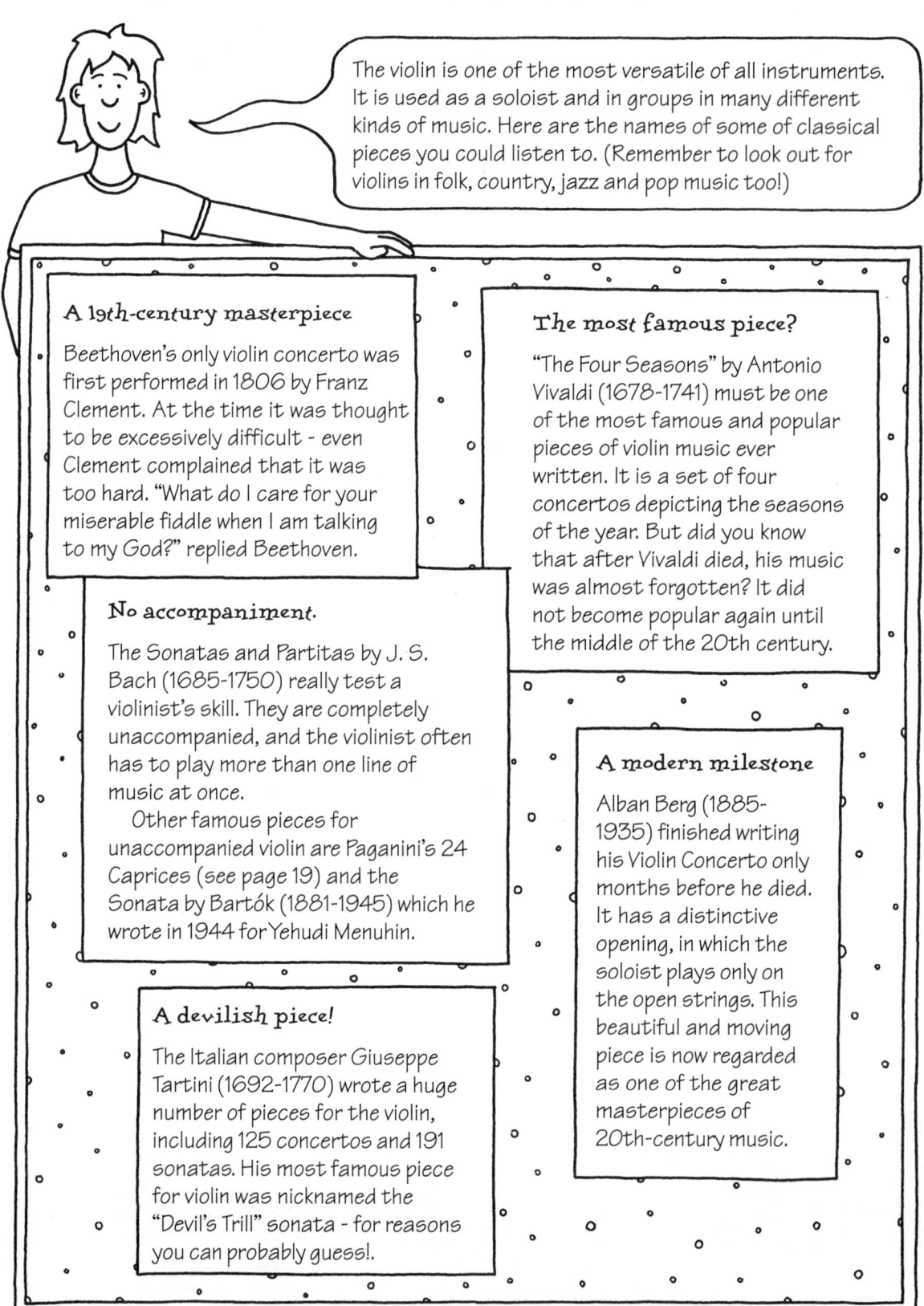

The violin is one of the most versatile of all instruments. It is used as a soloist and in groups in many different kinds of music. Here are the names of some of classical pieces you could listen to. (Remember to look out for violins in folk, country, jazz and pop music too!)

A 19th-century masterpiece

Beethoven's only violin concerto was first performed in 1806 by Franz Clement. At the time it was thought to be excessively difficult - even Clement complained that it was too hard. "What do I care for your miserable fiddle when I am talking to my God?" replied Beethoven.

No accompaniment.

The Sonatas and Partitas by J. S. Bach (1685-1750) really test a violinist's skill. They are completely unaccompanied, and the violinist often has to play more than one line of music at once.

Other famous pieces for unaccompanied violin are Paganini's 24 Caprices (see page 19) and the Sonata by Bartók (1881-1945) which he wrote in 1944 for Yehudi Menuhin.

A devilish piece!

The Italian composer Giuseppe Tartini (1692-1770) wrote a huge number of pieces for the violin, including 125 concertos and 191 sonatas. His most famous piece for violin was nicknamed the "Devil's Trill" sonata - for reasons you can probably guess!.

The most famous piece?

"The Four Seasons" by Antonio Vivaldi (1678-1741) must be one of the most famous and popular pieces of violin music ever written. It is a set of four concertos depicting the seasons of the year. But did you know that after Vivaldi died, his music was almost forgotten? It did not become popular again until the middle of the 20th century.

A modern milestone

Alban Berg (1885-1935) finished writing his Violin Concerto only months before he died. It has a distinctive opening, in which the soloist plays only on the open strings. This beautiful and moving piece is now regarded as one of the great masterpieces of 20th-century music.

More things to listen to...

SHOWPIECES:
There are many great pieces for violin soloists. Some show off the player's technique, like the concertos by Tchaikovsky or Max Bruch. Others, such as the sonata by Brahms and the concerto by Elgar, feature the instrument's beautiful tone. Why not listen to some of these pieces? You might also like to try "The Lark Ascending", a piece by Ralph Vaughan Williams for solo violin and orchestra.

ORCHESTRAL MUSIC:
Almost all orchestral pieces contain interesting parts for violin. For example, listen to the "Brandenburg Concertos" by Bach, Mozart's "Eine kleine Nachtmusik", or a symphony by Brahms. Barber's "Adagio for Strings" is a good example from the 20th century.

CHAMBER MUSIC:
Chamber music is music for a small number of instruments, such as string quartets - pieces for two violins, viola and cello. (See the puzzle below to find out more about these.)

Other chamber music with a part for violin includes the "Archduke" trio by Beethoven, Schubert's Octet, and the Nonet by Spohr. Modern examples include Stravinsky's "L'Histoire du Soldat" for violin, piano and clarinet and Messiaen's "Quatuor pour la fin du temps" for clarinet, violin, cello and piano.

Quick Scramble!

Rearrange these anagrams to find the names of composers who wrote famous string quartets!

AVSHOOTSCHIK   LAGER   BREWEN   SHRAMB

EVENBEHOT   KARTBO   BUTCHERS

DYNAH   GREENCHOBS   TRAMZO   BYUSSED

Timeline 1929-1953

1929 The Wall Street Crash hits New York.

1931 The Rickenbacker company makes the first electric guitar.

1935 Berg completes his Violin Concerto.

1936 Sergei Prokofiev composes a work for narrator and orchestra called 'Peter and the Wolf'.

1938 A Hungarian named Biro invents a new kind of ballpoint pen.

1945 The Second World War ends. Fighting began six years earlier when Germany invaded Poland.

1946 The first electronic computer is built.

1947 An aeroplane flies at supersonic speeds for the first time.

1953 Mount Everest is successfully climbed for the first time.

A violinist's life.

Fame and fortune, or hard work and stage fright? What is it like to be a violinist?

It must be great being a professional violinist. I mean, what an easy way to earn a living!

Not exactly. It involves lots of hard work and practice. Professional players often have to learn difficult new music very quickly, and they are always under pressure to play perfectly. Whether soloists, chamber musicians or orchestral players, professional violinists never have a particularly easy life.

But it's a good way of becoming rich and famous . . .

Only a handful of violinists become world-famous, like Paganini in the 19th century and Jascha Heifetz, Itzhak Perlman, Nigel Kennedy and others in the 20th. But even some of the most famous players of all time had to have other jobs as well, like teaching or composing.

I suppose you must get to see the world and meet really interesting people.

Yes, often. The best soloists get the opportunity to work with the finest conductors and orchestras. And some famous players have had close working relationships with composers - for example, Joachim and Brahms, and Oistrakh and Shostakovich. But the travel is tiring, and touring musicians get little time off between concerts and recording sessions.

So what jobs do violinists do?

All kinds of things - they work as soloists, in orchestras, as session musicians (playing on pop songs, film soundtracks and so on) and as teachers. But of course, not everyone wants to make a career in music - many people would rather play the violin as a hobby than as a job!

Quick Wordsearch!

Here are the names of some of the most famous violinists of all time. Cross off each one as you find it in the grid and then collect the remaining letters to find the name of another violinist and the title of his best known composition for violin.

```
I L L E T A C O L V I V W I
A L S I D I V I O T T I C N
T H I P N H N S E F E P O A
R E N N O I O T U N N E R I
E I I A T H N R I R R R E N
L F C R U G R A P P E L L I
S E A D S E W K G E T M L M
I T R I A S R H S A S A I E
E Z E N K E Y A S Y R N S G
R O V I E U X T E M P S N S
K J O A C H I M E N U H I N
```

Leopold **AUER**
Arcangelo **CORELLI**
Francesco **GEMINIANI**
Stephane **GRAPPELLI**
Jascha **HEIFETZ**
Joseph **JOACHIM**
Fritz **KREISLER**
Pietro **LOCATELLI**
Yehudi **MENUHIN**
Pietro **NARDINI**
David **OISTRAKH**
Niccolò **PAGANINI**
Itzhak **PERLMAN**
Ludwig **SPOHR**
Isaac **STERN**
Giuseppe **TARTINI**
Francesco **VERACINI**
Henri **VIEUXTEMPS**
Giovanni **VIOTTI**
Henryk **WIENIAWSKI**
Eugène **YSAYE**

The mystery violinist is ....
His famous composition is ....

Really BAD Ideas!

There are lots of great things to do with a violin, but this is <u>not</u> one of them.

4. Leaving it lying around.

Timeline 1954-1995

1954 Roger Bannister becomes the first person to run a mile in less than four minutes.

1957 In Liverpool, a new pop group called 'The Beatles' is formed.

1961 Yuri Gagarin makes the first space flight.

1963 Violinist Yehudi Menuhin opens a music school for gifted children.

1967 American composer Steve Reich writes a piece called 'Violin Phase'.

1982 The first compact discs are produced.

1985 British scientists discover a hole in the ozone layer above Antarctica.

1989 Uprisings begin in Eastern Europe. The Berlin Wall comes down.

1995 The Channel Tunnel is officially opened.

What can I do next?

Hints to help you become a better violinist, plus fun ideas and things to do.

Listen!

One of the best ways to become a good musician is to surround yourself with lots of music. It doesn't really matter what you choose - just listen to as much as you can.

If you ever get the chance to go and hear live music - take it! Live performances are more fun than concerts on TV or radio, and more inspiring too.

Practise!

If you want to become a really good violinist, the most important thing to do is *practise*. Set a regular time each day and try to stick to it - even if you'd rather be doing something else!

(Remember, it's a lot more useful to work for a short time once or twice a day than it is to have one long session a week.)

Record!

Why not try making a recording of your playing? When you play it back, listen carefully and ask yourself:

- "what do I like and dislike?"
- "how could I make it more interesting?"

Then, do some more practice, make another recording, and see if you can hear the difference next time!

Create!

Why not have a go at making up some violin music of your own? You could write some simple tunes and play them by yourself or with a group of friends.

Run out of ideas...?

You could also try playing along with your tapes or CDs. First, see if you can work out how to play the tunes. Then, try improvising using other notes as well.

Perform!

Playing in front of other people can be a nerve-wracking experience, but it's a very important part of becoming a good musician.

Why not get used to performing, by giving concerts for your family and friends? You should soon find that you start to feel much more confident!

...not for long!

Aim high!

No matter how long you've been playing the violin or how good you are, it's very important to always have something to aim for. It might be a concert, an exam, or just being able to play a piece you always thought was too difficult. Whatever it is, be ambitious - it's surprising what you can achieve when you really try!

It's important to spend time practising on your own, but it's also a good idea to play with other musicians whenever you can. Why not play duets with your friends, join an orchestra, or even start your own group? It doesn't matter what you play, as long as you enjoy it!

Quick Quiz!

Time for a quiz! Don't worry if the questions seem a bit tricky - you can find all the answers in the timeline on pages 7 to 23. Once you've finished, write down the first letter of each of the answers to find the name of a musical group you might like to join. What is it?

The hidden musical group is a ....
....

1 What was the first name of the first man in space?
2 Which sporting event first took place in 776 B.C.?
3 What began in Eastern Europe in 1989?
4 Who revolutionised the design of the violin bow?
5 What nationality was the inventor of the ballpoint pen?

6 Which instrument was invented in around 250 B.C.?
7 Which composer wrote a piece called 'Violin Phase'?
8 What did Ludwig Spohr invent in the early 1800s?
9 .... Lippershey invented the telescope in 1608.
10 What did dinosaurs become in around 65 million B.C.?
11 What was the first name of jazz violinist Grappelli?
12 Who finished composing a violin concerto in 1878?
13 Which company made the first electric guitar?
14 What did people begin to use in around 1,600 B.C.?

 Did you know that there are violin societies all over the world? They organise events, give out information and lots more. So why not join one?

Really BAD Ideas!

There are lots of great things to do with a violin, but this is <u>not</u> one of them . . .

5. Getting it wet.

Problems and advice.

Worried? Need someone to talk to? Then this is definitely the page for you!

Tuning trouble.

Q: My violin keeps going out of tune - why is this?

A: Remember that your violin is very sensitive. If you have very hot hands, or if you take it from a cold place into a warm one, you will probably need to adjust the tuning quite often anyway - don't worry about this. But if the tuning is really wobbly, there could be something wrong with your instrument. The strings may not be properly wound onto the pegs - ask your teacher to have a look and see if this is the case. If this doesn't solve the problem, take the violin to an instrument repairer who will check over the bridge, tailpiece and neck for you.

Soundhole slip-up.

Q: I've dropped something down the soundhole and it won't come out!

A: Whatever you do, don't poke around inside your violin! Turn it upside down, grip it firmly, and GENTLY shake it. If you can hear the something moving about, you may be able to roll it out of the hole. If you can't hear it moving, go to a repairer who will have the right tools for the job.

Aching arms

Q: After I've been playing for a while, I get pains - sometimes in my arms, sometimes my back, my shoulder and my neck. What's wrong?

A: Take lots of rests when you practise, especially if you are getting pains. Don't ever force yourself to play if it hurts. It may be that you aren't relaxed, or that you grip the violin or the bow too tightly. Tell your teacher, who should know if you need to change something about the way you play or stand. Don't worry if changing feels a bit strange at first - it's because you're asking your muscles to do different things. In the end, you will feel more comfortable when you play.

Balding bow.

Q: Why does the hair on my bow keep falling out?

A: It's perfectly natural for one or two hairs to break from time to time. Carefully cut broken hairs off, leaving a little spare at each end. Don't pull them out - this weakens the glue and the whole lot could come loose! If lots of hairs are breaking, check that you aren't tightening your bow too much.

Practice problems!

Q: My teacher says I don't practise properly, but I don't know what she means. I usually play my pieces at least once a day. What else am I meant to do?

A: When you practise, it can be tempting to play your pieces straight through, ignoring your mistakes. To practise properly, you need to focus on the things you find hard and keep working at them until you get them right.

Nasty nerves!

Q: I've been asked to play a solo in the school concert next week but I'm really nervous. What if I play lots of wrong notes?

A: Feeling nervous is normal - in fact it can even help you play better! Before the concert, give a mini-performance for your friends to practise playing in front of people. If you play a wrong note, carry on as if nothing had happened - if you don't look worried, most people won't notice! On the day, take time to relax and breathe deeply. And smile - you might even enjoy it!

Excuses, excuses...

Have you ever forgotten to do your practice and had to think up an excuse to get out of trouble? It seems that lots of people have! We asked your teachers to tell us some of the excuses they'd been given, and here are the things they said.

"I couldn't practise my violin because...

- ... my dad used the bow to unblock the drains and it went all soggy."
- ... the neighbours kept complaining."
- ... my toe hurt."
- ... my pet cockroach crawled into a soundhole and wouldn't come out."
- ... the weather wasn't very nice."
- ... it broke while I was playing tennis with it."

The violin A to Z.

A set of violin facts - some interesting, some fun, and some downright silly!

A is for A............
The name of a very well-known family of Italian violin makers?

B is for B............
The surname of Max, composer of a concerto for violin?

C is for c............
What your teacher will be if you don't do your practice?!

D is for d............
The lowest-pitched member of the violin family?

E is for E............
The country where the 'masenqo' is most often played?

F is for f............
What a tadpole turns into . . . or part of a bow?

G is for g............
Sometimes used to make the insides of violin strings?

H is for H............
The name of a kind of fiddle played in parts of Norway?

I is for i............
If you practise every day, your playing will soon do this?!

J is for j............
Stephane Grappelli is famous for this kind of music?

K is for K............
Surname of Fritz - Austrian violinist and composer?

L is for l............
The Italian word 'forte' tells you to play like this?

M is for m............
An instrument also known as the horse-head fiddle?

N is for n............
How you might feel before playing in an important concert?

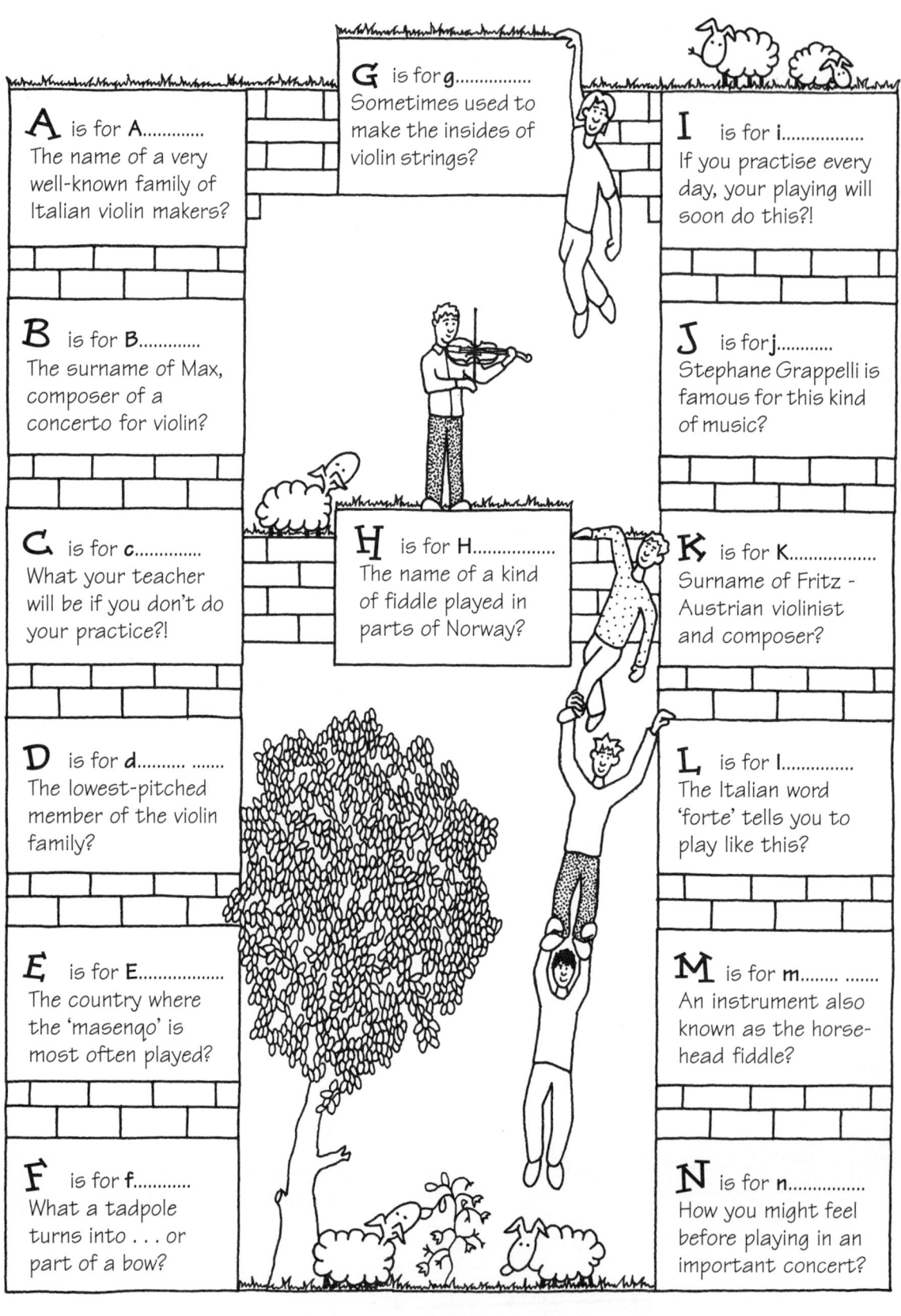

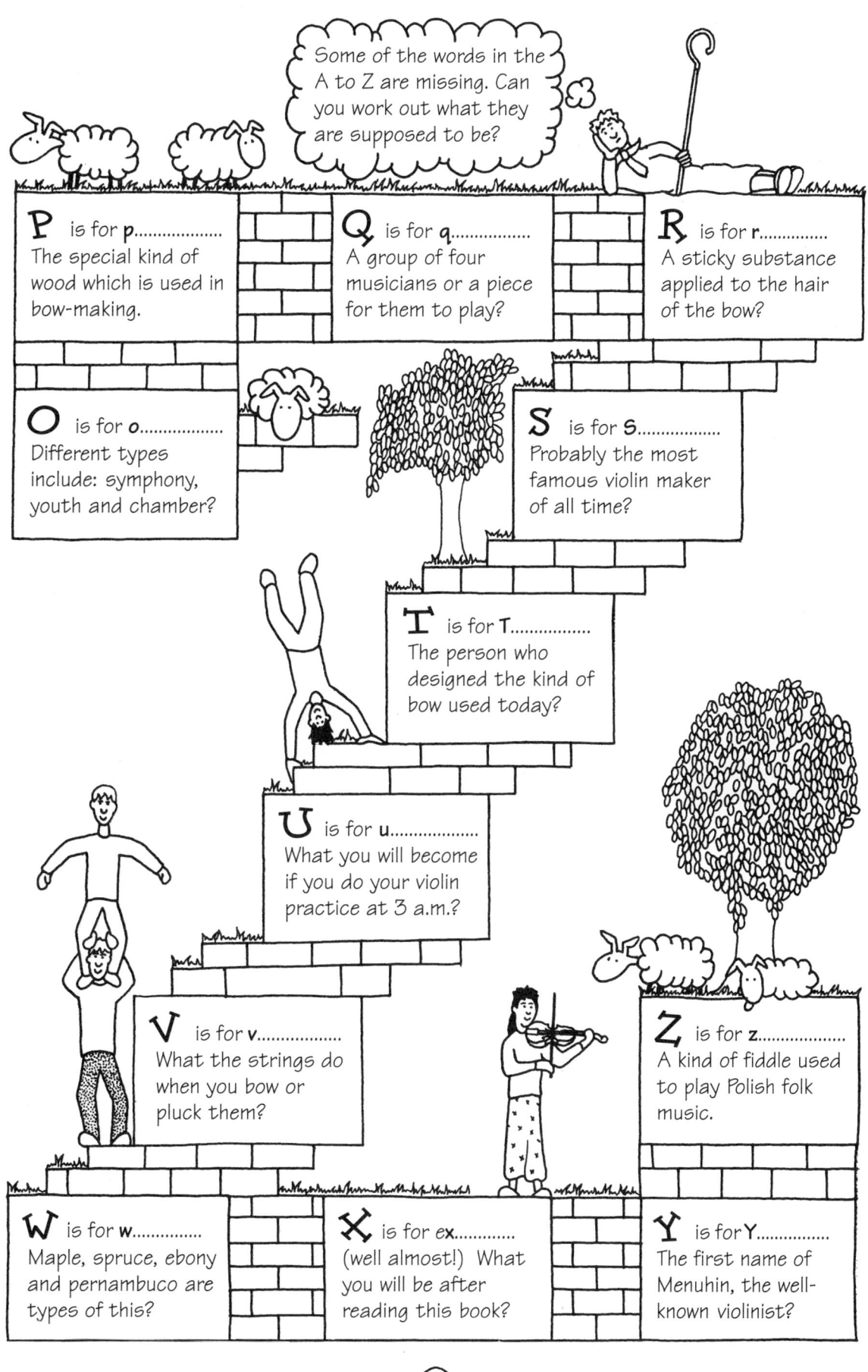

Useful information.

A guide to some of the most common words and signs used in music.

Notes

- o   A **semibreve** or **whole note**. Worth 4 counts.
- 𝅗𝅥   A **minim** or **half note**. Worth 2 counts.
- ♩   A **crotchet** or **quarter note**. Worth 1 count.
- ♪   A **quaver** or **eighth note**. Worth ½ count.
- 𝅘𝅥𝅯   A **semiquaver** or **sixteenth note**. Worth ¼ count.

Rests

- —   A **semibreve** or **whole note rest**. Worth 4 counts.
- —   A **minim** or **half note rest**. Worth 2 counts.
- 𝄽   A **crotchet** or **quarter note rest**. Worth 1 count.
- 𝄾   A **quaver** or **eighth note rest**. Worth ½ count.
- 𝄿   A **semiquaver** or **sixteenth note rest**. Worth ¼ count.

 If you want to know more about how to read and write music, why not try the Theory Fun Factory books? You'll find them in all good music shops!

Tempo markings

presto	fast
allegro	quick, lively
allegretto	quite quick
moderato	at a moderate speed
andante	at a walking pace
lento	slow
accelerando	get gradually faster
rallentando	get gradually slower
ritardando	get gradually slower
M.M. ♩ = 132	a metronome mark

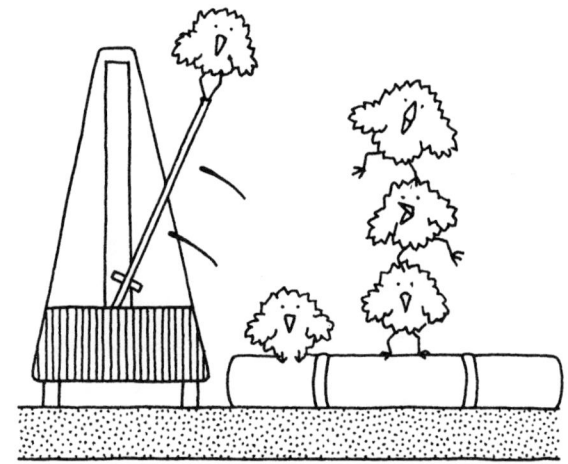

 Did you know that the letters M.M. are short for 'Maelzel's metronome'? (Johann Maelzel was the man who patented the metronome in 1814.)

Musical signs

♯ - A **sharp** sign. Raises the pitch of the note which follows it by a semitone.
♭ - A **flat** sign. Lowers the pitch of the note which follows it by a semitone.
♮ - A **natural** sign. Cancels sharp and flat signs earlier in the music.
𝄞 - A **treble clef**. Used in music for high voices or instruments - e.g. flute.
𝄢 - A **bass clef**. Used in music for low voices or instruments - e.g. bassoon.

Dynamics

fortissimo (ff)	very loud
forte (f)	loud
mezzo forte (mf)	quite loud
mezzo piano (mp)	quite quiet
piano (p)	quiet
pianissimo (pp)	very quiet
crescendo	get gradually louder
diminuendo	get gradually quieter
decrescendo	get gradually quieter

More words and signs

⊓ - tells you to play using a down bow.
∨ - tells you to play using an up bow.
The word **pizzicato** tells you to pluck the string instead of bowing it.
The word **arco** tells you to start using the bow again, after playing *pizzicato*.
A **staccato** sign (a dot above or below a note) means 'make the note a little shorter than usual'.
The word **legato** means 'play smoothly.'

 Another Italian term which you may find in your violin music is **con legno**. This tells you to play using the wood of the bow instead of the hair!

Time signatures

Signs like $\frac{3}{2}$ and $\frac{3}{4}$ are called time signatures. The top number tells you how many beats there are in a bar, the bottom number tells you what kind of beat. For example:

$\frac{3}{2}$ = three ♩ beats per bar

$\frac{4}{4}$ = four ♩ beats per bar

$\frac{6}{8}$ = six ♪ beats per bar

𝐂 = another way of writing $\frac{4}{4}$

Musical moods

agitato	agitated
amoroso	loving
cantabile	in a singing style
dolce	sweet
espressivo	expressive
furioso	furious
giocoso	playful, merry
grazioso	graceful
grave	very slow, solemn
maestoso	majestic
vivace	lively

 The practice of using words to describe how music should sound began in Italy in the 17th century. That's why many musical words are written in Italian.

Really BAD Ideas!

There are lots of great things to do with a violin, but this is <u>not</u> one of them...

6. Dropping it...

The back page.

Can't find what you're looking for? Maybe an index and answers section will help!

Index

accessories, 12
bow, 3, 7, 11, 17, 26
bowing, 31
bridge, 3, 7, 8
cello, 4, 5
chin rest, 3, 11, 12, 17
Cremona, 16
double bass, 5
folk fiddles, 6
jazz, 5, 19
lira da braccio, 16
materials used (in violin making), 3, 7, 9, 11
orchestra, 4, 5, 19, 21, 22
Paganini, 18, 19, 20, 22

repertoire for violin, 18, 19, 20, 21
scroll, 3, 9, 10, 11
Stradivari, 16, 17
string quartet, 4, 5, 19, 21
strings, 3, 4, 5, 6, 7, 8, 12, 16, 20
sympathetic strings, 6, 7
Tourte, 17
varnish, 10, 16
viol, 16, 18
viola, 4, 5
violinists, 18, 19, 20, 22, 23
violoncello, see cello

Answers

p.6   1. Wang-pi 2. Kamancha 3. Sarinda
      4. Er-hu 5. Lira 6. Zlobocki 7. Masenqo
p.11 Maple, Spruce, Ebony, Horse, Pernambuco, Plastic
p.13 Jenny, 13, Rosin; Marco, 10, Duster; Richard, 8, Bow; Dominique, 11, Violin
p.15 Tartini
p.18 18th, centuries, grew, skillful, demanding, Violinists, Paganini, audiences, concerts, playing, fashionable, violin
p.21 Shostakovich, Elgar, Webern, Brahms, Beethoven, Bartók, Schubert, Haydn, Schoenberg, Mozart, Debussy
p.23 Vivaldi; The Four Seasons
p.25 Youth orchestra
pp.28-29 Amati, Bruch, cross, double bass, Ethiopia, frog, glissando, Hardanger, improve, jazz, Kreisler, loudly, morin khuur, nervous, orchestra, pernambuco, quartet, rosin, Stradivari, Tourte, unpopular, vibrate, wood, expert, Yehudi, zlobocki

Thank yous...

• With thanks to: Pam Elliott (Research), Alastair Laing (Additional Research), and Ian Martin (Additional Research and Design).
• Many thanks also to: Paul Bowers, Rachel Douglas and Edward Huws Jones.
• And special thanks to: Dominique Collyer, Kelly Maddick, Betsy Porritt, Emma Robinson and Jenny Tamplin (Fun Factory Readers).

THE END!